Butterflies

by Ciara Healy

Embracing Extinction I

All I ever wanted, all I ever needed is here in my arms I

Res Familiares I

Since it was not home strangeness made sense I

Since it was not home strangeness made sense II

Res Familiares II

Nocturna I

Replica

Transitus Patria (Migrant Journeys) I

Nocturna II

proboscis

cell

veins

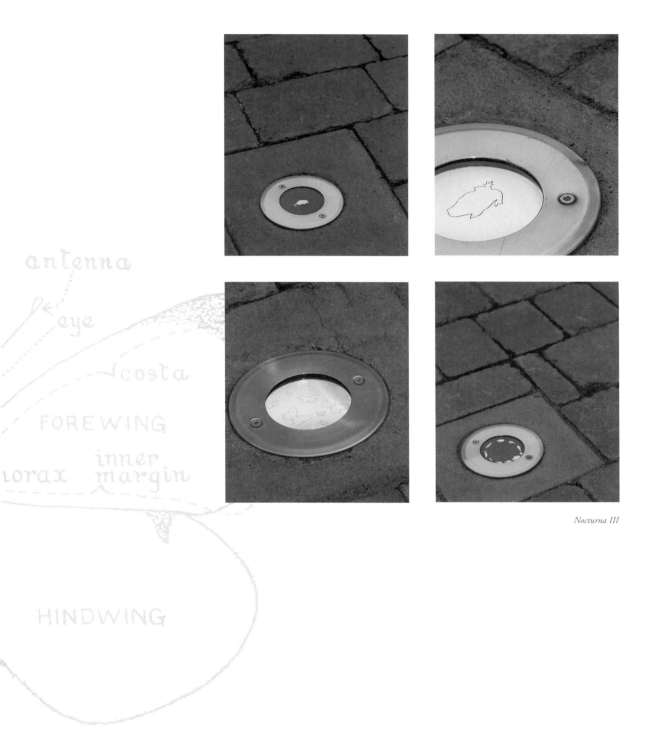

antenna

eye

costa

FOREWING

inner
margin

thorax

HINDWING

Nocturna III

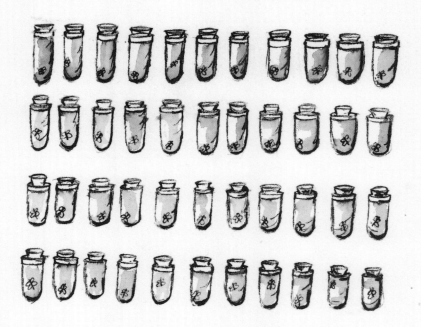

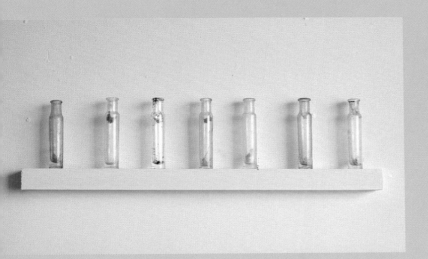

Its nothing to you but it keeps me alive

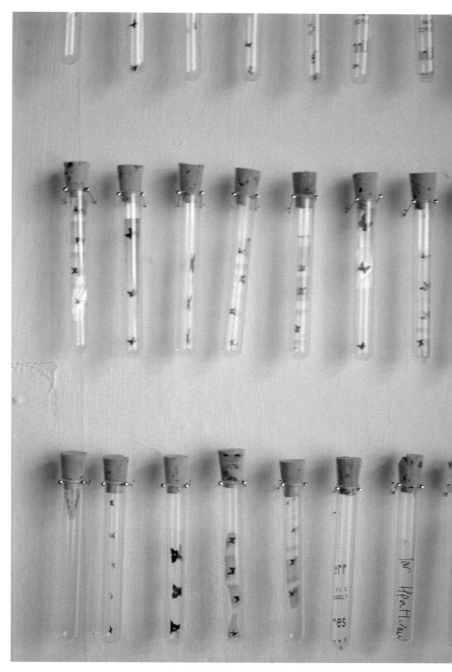

Archives of the Lost

Embracing Extinction II

Study for Replica

Papiers

Transitus Patria (Migrant Journeys) II

The fyrthe Dike

PART OF

Charters

Mepole

Fen

Fen

THE ISLE

Somershā
parke

Colne

Transitus Patria (Migrant Journeys) III

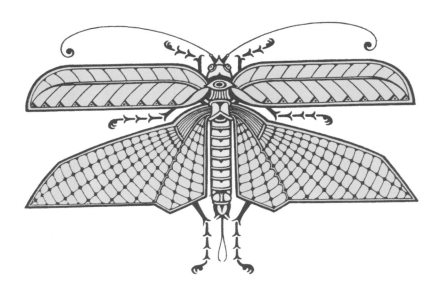

Que – reste –t'il de nos amours? I

If I could have held you once more in that light

Res Familiares (detail)

Archives of the Lost II

Res Familiares (detail)

...la chère visage de ma jeunesse

All I ever wanted, allI ever needed is here in my arms II

Res Familiares (detail)

Que – reste –t'il de nos amours? II

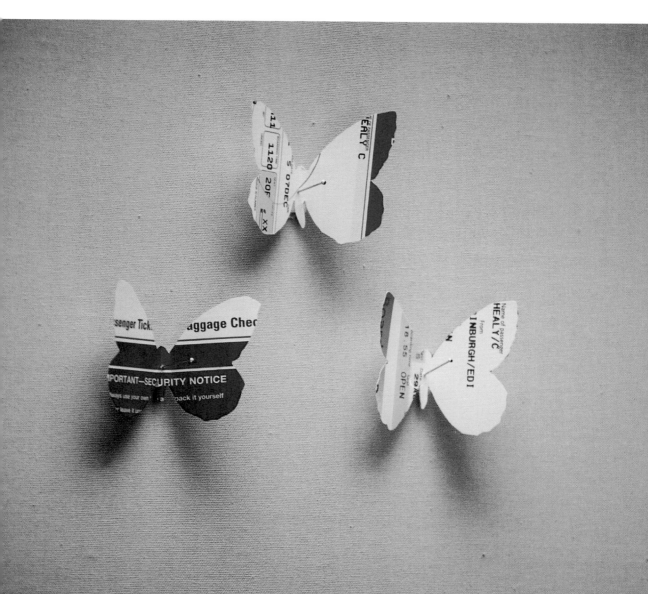

Un paysage, si bien caché

53

I really miss you

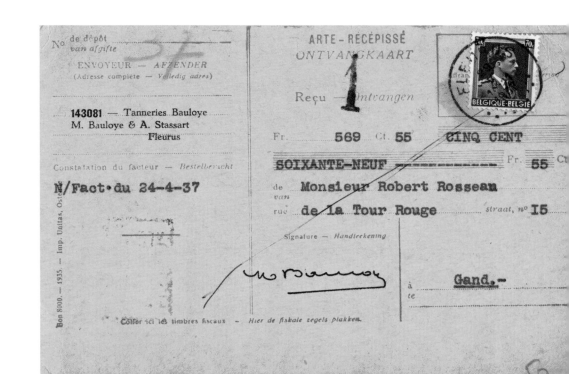

No de dépôt
van afgifte

ENVOYEUR — *AFZENDER*
(Adresse complète — *Volledig adres*)

143081 — Tanneries Bauloye
M. Bauloye & A. Stassart
Fleurus

Constatation du facteur — *Bestelbericht*

N/Fact•du 24-4-37

Bon 8000. — 1935. — Imp. Unitas, Ost.

Coller ici les timbres fiscaux — *Hier de fiskale zegels plakken.*

ARTE - RÉCÉPISSÉ
ONTVANGKAART

Reçu — *Ontvangen*

1

Fr.   **569**   Ct. **55**   CINQ CENT

SOIXANTE-NEUF   Fr. **55** Ct.

de   Monsieur Robert Rosseau
van

rue   de la Tour Rouge   *straat*, n° **15**

Signature — *Handteekening*

à   Gand.—
te

BELGIQUE-BELGIE

50

Rendered Still

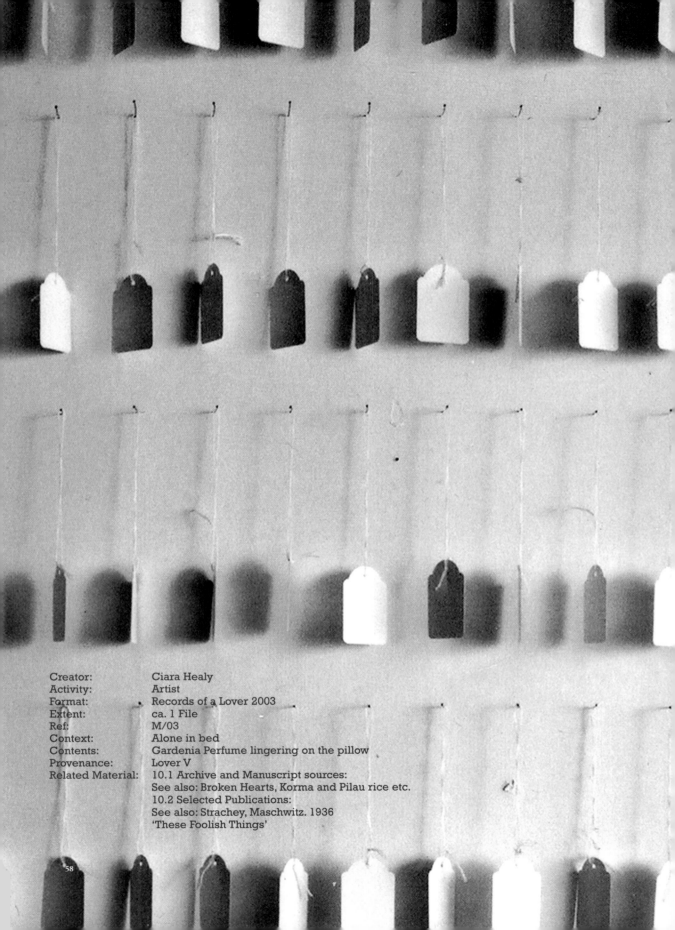

Creator: Ciara Healy
Activity: Artist
Format: Records of a Lover 2003
Extent: ca. 1 File
Ref: M/03
Context: Alone in bed
Contents: Gardenia Perfume lingering on the pillow
Provenance: Lover V
Related Material: 10.1 Archive and Manuscript sources:
                    See also: Broken Hearts, Korma and Pilau rice etc.
                    10.2 Selected Publications:
                    See also: Strachey, Maschwitz. 1936
                    'These Foolish Things'

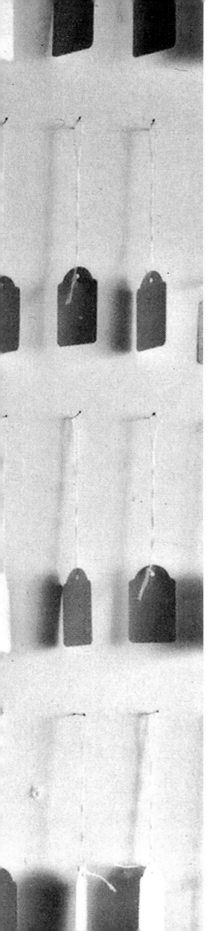

Embracing Extinction	Golden Thread Gallery, Belfast; exh: *One Place Twice*	2003
All I ever wanted, all I ever needed is here in my arms	5th Guinness StoreHouse, Dublin; exh: *Tripswitch*	2003
Res Familiares	The Natural History Musuem, Dublin; exh: *Res Familiares*	2002
Since it was not home strangeness made sense	Sligo Art Gallery, Sligo; exh: *Iontas*	2005
Nocturna	OPW Permanent Public Art Commission Dublin Zoo, exh: *Nocturna Archives*	2004
Replica	South Tipperary Arts Centre, Co Tipperary; exh: *Replica,* (in collaboration with Ann Mulrooney)	2005
Transitus Patria (Migrant Journeys)	Wicklow County Council, Wicklow; exh: *Group Show*	2006
Its nothing to you but it keeps me alive	Work in Progress, Studio	2003
Archives of the Lost	Ulster Museum, Belfast; exh: *The Suicide of Objects*	2004
The Ghost of you clings	Signal Arts Centre, Bray; exh: *Pin*	2004
Little counsels for the sanctification and happiness of everyday life	Naughton Gallery, Queens University, Belfast; exh: *Revealing Objects*	2003
Papiers	Form Gallery, Cork; exh: *Form Group Show*	2004
Que – reste –t'il de nos amours?	Dublin Fringe Festival, (Various Venues), Dublin; exh: *Shift*	2002
If I could have held you once more in that light	Work in Progress, Studio	2003
…la chère visage de ma jeunesse	Dublin Fringe Festival, (Various Venues), Dublin; exh: *Shift*	2002
Un paysage, si bien caché	Dublin Fringe Festival, (Various Venues), Dublin; exh: *Shift*	2002
I really miss you	Goethe Institut, Dublin; exh: *The National Gallery*	2003
Rendered Still	Ulster Museum, Belfast; exh: *The Suicide of Objects*	2004

Title of image on p.18 & 19: **The Ghost of you clings,** p.20: *Little counsels for the sanctification and happiness of everyday life,* p.22 & 23: **Nocturna IV,** p.26: **Replica** and p.30 & 31: **Papiers** (Detail).

Ciara Healy is an artist, writer and curator based in Ireland. She has exhibited extensively in several solo and group shows including solo site-specific projects with the Natural History Museum, Dublin and OPW Public Art Commissions for Dublin Zoo. Her curatorial projects have taken place at the Lewis Glucksman Gallery, Cork, The National Irish Visual Arts Library NCAD, Dublin and the Dublin Fringe Festival. Healy is a member and curator for the artists group Pin. She has published essays on visual art for numerous catalogues and journals. Her work is represented in public and private collections in Ireland, Belgium, the UK and the US.

All my love and thanks to Andrew Kelly. A special thanks to Dara Ní Bheacháin.

Photographs of Nocturna by Ros Kavanagh, 2004.

Photographs of Embracing Extinction by Louisa Sloan, 2003.

This book was printed by Glennon Print using Garamond & Rockwell fonts.

This book was published by www.ignition.ie and designed by Dara Ní Bheacháin.

ISBN 0-9552256-4-7